Dr. Kate

i

Badger Biographies

Other Badger Biographies

Belle & Bob La Follette: Partners in Politics
Caroline Quarlls and the Underground Railroad
Casper Jaggi: Master Swiss Cheese Maker
Curly Lambeau: Building the Green Bay Packers
Harley and the Davidsons: Motorcycle Legends
Mai Ya's Long Journey
Mountain Wolf Woman: A Ho-Chunk Girlhood
Ole Evinrude and His Outboard Motor
A Recipe for Success: Lizzie Kander and Her Cookbook
Tents, Tigers, and the Ringling Brothers

Dr. Kate
ANGEL ON SNOWSHOES

REBECCA HOGUE WOJAHN

WISCONSIN HISTORICAL SOCIETY PRESS

Published by the Wisconsin Historical Society Press
Publishers since 1855

©2009 by State Historical Society of Wisconsin

wisconsin history.org

Printed in the United States of America
Designed by Jill Bremigan

13 12 11 10 09   1 2 3 4 5

Library of Congress Cataloging-in-Publication Data

Wojahn, Rebecca Hogue.
  Dr. Kate : angel on snowshoes / Rebecca Hogue Wojah.
    p. cm. — (Badger biographies)
  Includes bibliographical references and index.
  ISBN 978-0-87020-421-0 (pbk. : alk. paper) 1. Newcomb, Kate Pelham, 1886–1956—Juvenile literature. 2. Women physicians—Wisconsin—Biography—Juvenile literature. I. Title.
  R692.N49 2009
  610.82092—dc22
  [B]
                        2008043263

For Don, Carl, and Eli

Publication of this book is made possible, in part, by a gift from
Mrs. Harvey E. Vick of Milwaukee, Wisconsin.

Contents

Dr. Kate often traveled on snowshoes to visit patients.

1

Kate Asks "Why?"

In the dark cold of the night, Dr. Kate's phone rang. Somewhere out in the winter woods of northern Wisconsin, someone needed a doctor. Dr. Kate pulled on her boots, grabbed her medical bag, and headed out. It didn't matter how far the journey or how late the hour. Dr. Kate was always willing to help.

One night, a snowstorm blew so hard that Dr. Kate rode to her patient in a snowplow instead of her car. When the plow slid off the road, she strapped on her snowshoes and hiked 2 more miles through the storm. She arrived at the cabin just in time to save a new mother's life. Only then did Dr. Kate tend to her own stinging legs, **frostbitten** from her snowy hike.

Another time, the creek was the fastest **route**. But chunks of jagged ice still crowded the water. Dr. Kate's canoe bumped

frostbitten: damaged by extreme cold   **route**: the places a doctor or delivery person goes each day in the same order

1

and scraped as it moved through the water. Then it started sinking. But Dr. Kate didn't let that stop her either. She stepped right out into the icy creek and waded to shore. Nothing got between her and someone in need.

Growing up, nobody would have ever imagined that quiet Kate Pelham would become the snowshoeing doctor of **rural**

northern Wisconsin. Back then, girls were expected to get married and have children. But not Kate. At least, that's not *all* she wanted.

Kate was born in 1885 or 1886 in **Leoti**, Kansas, a small town on the **prairie**. Her mother, who was also named Kate, stayed home with her. Her father, Tom, worked at the bank in town. When she was just 4 years old, her mother and new baby brother died as her mother gave birth.

Kate Pelham, age 4, in Leoti, Kansas.

rural: in the countryside or on a farm   **prairie** (**prair** ree): a large area of flat or rolling grassland with few or no trees   **Leoti** (lee **oh** tuh)

Kate was **devastated**. She couldn't understand where they had gone. For days, she waited on the porch for her mother to return. When she finally realized her mother wasn't coming back, Kate wanted to know why. *Why* did her mother and brother have to die? That awful feeling stuck with Kate her whole life.

After her mother's death, Kate's grandparents moved to Leoti to be with Kate and her father. In 1890, a tornado hit Leoti. While Kate's house was fine, much of the town was flattened. Kate longed to help all those people who had lost their homes and farms. The next time she visited her father at his bank, she stuffed money inside her **muff** and walked out. After a panicked search, the money was discovered under the Pelhams' living room rug: $30,000! Kate explained that she took the money to help families who had lost their homes in the tornado. Already she was showing the **compassion** that would make her such a caring doctor later in life.

devastated (**dev** uh stay tud): very upset, shocked   **muff**: a tube-like item of clothing, often lined with fur, that girls put their hands inside to keep warm   **compassion** (kuhm **pash** uhn): a strong desire to help someone in need

Just months after her mother's death, Kate's father got married again. Kate and her new stepmother, Nona, did not get along very well. When her new brothers and sisters started arriving, Kate was pushed into the background. During this time, Kate's father was very busy studying. He was training to become a lawyer. He was so busy, he didn't have much time for Kate. Then the family moved from Kansas to Buffalo, New York, so that he could begin to **practice** law. The move meant Kate had to leave her grandparents behind. Leaving them in Leoti was another difficult loss for Kate.

Kate was very lonely, even though it was her job to look after all her brothers and sisters. The place where Kate was happiest was school. She had been reading since she was just 3 years old. In Buffalo, she attended elementary school and then high school. In high school, Kate was quiet and a good student. She also experienced her first heartbreak. When she was just 16 years old, she and a classmate, Robert, were secretly **engaged** to be married. But in their last year of high school, Robert died of **pneumonia**. Kate was stunned. It was even harder for Kate because they had kept their engagement

practice: to work at a profession, especially as a doctor or lawyer   **engaged**: promised to marry   **pneumonia** (nuh **mohn** yuh): a disease that causes the lungs to be filled with fluid, making breathing difficult

a secret. Her family and friends didn't realize just how serious she and Robert had become. So, all alone once again, Kate asked why. Why did Robert have to die—just like her mother and little brother?

Only this time, Kate had an idea. If she became a doctor, maybe she could help sick people so that they didn't *have* to die. It soon became the only thing Kate could think about. It was the thing she wanted most.

Kate's father, Tom Pelham, was a banker and a lawyer.

Being a doctor, however, was not a common **career** for a young woman 100 years ago. This was certainly something her father did not expect his daughter to become. According to Tom Pelham, medicine was "no profession of a lady." And since Kate needed her father to pay for her schooling, she had to push the idea to the back of her mind. Instead of medicine, she trained for one of the few careers that women were encouraged to go into: teaching.

career: a profession

5

Kate, her half-brother Charles Pelham, and a friend pose for a picture.

Kate (far left) and friends in Boston. Kate hated wearing the tight corset that squeezed her waist.

When she finished high school, Kate went to another year of school to become a teacher. Then she took a job teaching fifth and sixth grade in Buffalo. She liked working with the children, but she hated the constant challenge of getting the students to behave.

Meanwhile, her father was getting ready to move the family yet again. He had been offered an important position, to be the head of the **Gillette** Razor Company. That meant the family would have to move to Boston, Massachusetts. But since Kate had her own job, she decided to stay in Buffalo. Although she didn't like teaching, she had

Gillette (jil et)

6

finally found a place she belonged. She had fun singing in a quartet with her friends, and she became **involved** in the **Women's Christian Temperance Union**. She even had a few women friends who were doctors. They reminded Kate of her own dream.

Kate's contentment didn't last long. Just a few months after they left, her father wrote that her stepmother had passed away. He needed Kate to move to Boston and help run his home—and he hoped that Kate might find a husband in Boston. Though she wished she could stay in Buffalo, Kate headed to Massachusetts.

The Pelham residence in Boston, where Kate played hostess to her father's important guests.

There she took her place in her father's grand house as "Miss Kathleen." Because her father was not married, she often had to play **hostess** when wealthy people came for dinner.

involved: taking part in **Women's Christian Temperance** (**tem** pur ins) **Union**: a group of women that worked together to stop the selling and drinking of beer and liquor in the 1910s **hostess**: a woman who entertains guests

Inside, Kate was miserable. She always chose the wrong clothes. She didn't know how to dance. She did not agree that wine or alcohol should be served at dinners. She turned her wineglass upside down whenever wine was offered. **Small talk** at parties pained her. Life as a **socialite** pinched at Kate as much as the tight **corsets** and pointed slippers she now had to wear.

One night at an important dinner, **squab** was served. Kate stared at the tiny pigeon on her plate—how was she to eat it? She poked at it with her fork. Then she sliced it with her knife. Suddenly, it shot off her plate and skidded onto the floor! Kate's face bloomed red as everyone at the table watched the servants clean up.

Kate had had enough. The next day she told her father, "Papa, I'm sorry about what happened last night, but it couldn't be helped. This is the end. I can't stand this life any longer . . . I'm going to study medicine." She told him that if he refused to pay for her schooling, one of his business friends was ready to help.

small talk: talk about unimportant things   **socialite** (**soh** shuh lıt): a person well-known for wearing stylish clothing and giving and attending parties   **corset** (**kor** sit): a close-fitting garment worn under the clothes to support and shape the waist, hips, and breasts   **squab** (skwahb): a very young pigeon

Her father sighed. "That won't be necessary, Kate," he said. "I'll pay for your training myself. Perhaps I've been wrong in trying to force you into a pattern that is against your **nature**. I'm giving up."

With delight, Kate wrote to her friends in Buffalo that she was coming back. And coming back not to teach but to study to become a doctor!

Kate eagerly packed her things. But as she left her father's home, her father took her aside and said, "Katie, I hope when you become a doctor, you will be able to save other mothers from dying as your mother died." Finally, Kate knew that her father really did understand.

But little did he know that she would go on and do just that.

nature: the character of someone or something

2

Becoming a Doctor

Kate settled into **medical school** with great **gusto** in the fall of 1913. She was one of just 6 women in her class, but she was too excited to think about that. She was finally going to learn to be a doctor. In her classes, she studied hard. Medical school was not easy for Kate. However, she worked eagerly and soon became one of the best students in her class. Later in life, she often praised her professors at the University of Buffalo. They taught her the knowledge and

Kate (middle) and friends in Buffalo, New York, where Kate attended medical school.

medical school: school one attends to learn to be a doctor   **gusto** (**guhs** toh): joy or enthusiasm

skills she needed to become a doctor. They also taught her things that didn't come from books. "Whenever you enter a sick room, always enter with a prayer on your lips," one **professor** would always say. Dr. Kate remembered this for the rest of her career.

Kate was overjoyed to see her old friends in Buffalo. Though she was shy, she made many new friends at school. Soon, she had a whole circle of friends. She had one male friend, Pat, whom she liked as more than a friend. In fact, they decided their senior year of medical school to take the **trolley** downtown to the **city hall** and get married. But as they climbed the steps to the building, they realized that they had less than a dollar between them. A marriage license cost one dollar. Unhappily, they headed back home without going inside city hall.

It probably was best that Kate didn't marry Pat that day. As graduation got closer, he told her about his plan for their life together. After medical school, he planned to take an **internship** in a country town. Kate would stay home and

professor: a teacher of the highest rank at a college or university   **trolley**: an electric streetcar that runs on tracks and gets its power from an overhead wire   **city hall**: a public building used for government offices **internship**: the period of time that a new doctor spends working with more experienced doctors to prepare to practice medicine on his or her own

11

care for their house and babies. She was stunned. To give up being a doctor now after all her hard work? How could Pat even think of such a thing?

"But what about *my* internship?" she asked.

"One doctor in the family is enough," was Pat's reply.

Women in Medicine

Nowadays, people don't think twice about seeing a woman doctor. But when Dr. Kate became a doctor, it was very unusual. It had been just a little over 60 years since Elizabeth Blackwell became the very first woman doctor in the United States. Blackwell had **applied** to almost every medical school in the country, but none would **accept** her. She was turned down not because her grades weren't good enough but simply because she was female. "The **primary requisite** of a good surgeon is to be a man—a man of courage," Edmund Andrews, a well-known surgeon of the time, wrote in 1861. Most people agreed.

Finally, Elizabeth Blackwell was accepted at the Geneva Medical College in New York, but only because the school thought it was a joke. When she got there, the students and professors were

applied: asked to be allowed to attend a school or work at a job   **accept** (ak **sept**): to agree to let someone attend a school or start a job   **primary** (**prI** mair ree): most important   **requisite** (**rek** wuh zit): something someone must do or have; a requirement

horrified. Despite this, she went on to earn their respect. She finished at the top of her class.

After graduating, Blackwell started the New York **Infirmary** for Women and Children. It was the first hospital run by women. It was also the first to give medical training only to women. Soon other women-only medical schools were built around the country. As people saw women succeed as doctors, other women were finally allowed to enter regular medical schools. By 1900, the number of women doctors in America had grown to 7,000. In 1860, there had been only 200. Still, that was just a small portion of all the people who studied to become doctors.

Elizabeth Blackwell became the first woman doctor in the United States in 1849.

Just as Elizabeth Blackwell was a hero to Dr. Kate, Dr. Kate became a **role model** for the girls and women who came to her as patients. As more and more girls were treated by women doctors, they were encouraged to think they might become doctors, too. But it took almost 100 years more—until 2003—before women finally made up half of all medical students in the United States.

infirmary (in **furm** uh ree): a place where sick or hurt people are cared for, smaller than a hospital   **role model**: a person looked up to for his or her ability or experience

But one doctor in the family wasn't enough for Kate. She told Pat that she couldn't marry him; she was going to be a doctor. She began to study even harder. Pat was the one student whose grades were ahead of hers, and now that they weren't together, Kate wanted to do better than he did. She almost made it, too. She finished second in her class, less than one point behind Pat.

Kate became Dr. Kate in 1917, after graduating from the University of Buffalo Medical School at the age of 31.

Kate's scores were high enough to earn her an internship at the Women's Hospital in Detroit, Michigan, the following fall. During the internship, she would finish her training so that she could become an official doctor. For the summer, she took a job in New York City. She lived at the New York Infirmary for Women and Children, making **house calls** in the **tenement** neighborhoods of the Lower East Side in Manhattan. It was a poor neighborhood with many **immigrants**. Often,

house call: a visit by a doctor in someone's home   **tenement** (**ten** uh mint): a run-down building, especially one that is crowded and in a poor part of a city   **immigrant** (**im** uh grint): a person from one country who moves to settle permanently in another

Dr. Kate didn't speak the same language as her patients. But as she visited each home in the neighborhood, she soon became known as the "Lady Doc."

While at medical school, Dr. Kate had delivered her first baby—actually, *babies*. Her first delivery was a set of twins, much to Kate's and the mother's surprise. In New York, Dr. Kate got a lot more practice delivering babies. She made house calls at all hours of the day and night. That summer and fall, she delivered more than 800 babies in the cramped apartments of the neighborhood.

The tenement houses in New York where Kate first worked as a doctor were often crowded and dirty.

Once, when a very large baby was turned the wrong way, Dr. Kate warned the father that she didn't think the baby could survive the delivery. He turned on her. "You take care. If the baby dies, *you* die!" Dr. Kate's eyes widened, but she took her old professor's advice and started praying as she worked. It was a miracle that the baby lived. Later she said the experience made her trust her faith more.

In December of that year, Kate made her way to Detroit. Nothing could have been more different from New York's tenements. The Women's Hospital was **modern** and bright. Most of the patients were not poor. What's more, Kate would work with some of the best doctors in America.

Almost immediately, one of the doctors took a special interest in Kate. In fact, he wanted to marry her. But Kate still remembered Pat, so she ignored the new doctor. She didn't want to fall into another trap. Besides, Kate was having too much fun. There were three other women doctors on the staff at Women's Hospital. Dr. Kate and Dr. Grace Clark became such close friends that their coworkers called them

modern: up-to-date or new

"Kate and **Duplicate**." They said it so that "duplicate" rhymed with "Kate." When Kate finished her internship at Women's Hospital, she and the other three women doctors started their own **practice** in Detroit.

The Detroit Women's Hospital, where Dr. Kate was an intern, had up-to-date equipment like in this operating room.

duplicate (**doop** li kit): an exact copy of something, a double   **practice**: the business of a doctor or lawyer

Their new practice meant they had to get around the city with lightning speed. Both Kate and Grace decided it was time to own cars—and learn how to drive them. The car salesman and mechanic who sold them their cars, Bill Newcomb, offered to teach them how to drive. Kate was terrified at first, especially of busy city traffic. The only way to **overcome** her fear was to face it, so Bill drove her downtown. Then he stepped out of the car, right in the middle of the street! He said she would have to find her way home by herself or be stuck. He would walk home. By the time Kate returned home with the car, she had lost her fear of driving.

Learning to drive was a new experience for many people in the 1920s.

overcome: to deal with or get over a problem or feeling

Even after Kate and Grace learned to drive, they continued to be friends with Bill. Bill had grown up in the woods of Michigan. Although he had finished only grade school, he was smart and had read many books. And he was handsome. Kate was sure he must have liked Grace better, but Grace told her it wasn't true—Bill never said a word about love. Still, Kate decided to spend less time with Bill. Instead, she began to spend more time with the handsome doctor who had proposed to her when she first moved to Detroit.

A few months later, Grace became very ill. Despite the best medical care available at the time, her life faded away. Her death came as a shock to both Bill and Kate, and they pulled together in their grief. Soon Bill told her something that made her heart leap: he'd loved Kate all along. Once they realized that they both loved each other, Bill wanted to marry Kate. But the doctor from the Women's Hospital was still in her life. Kate didn't know what to do with two marriage **proposals**. She loved Bill's company, but a doctor for a husband would be a much better choice than a mechanic, wouldn't it? She decided to visit her family in Boston and let them help her decide.

proposal: an offer of marriage

Grandmother Pelham thought she should marry the doctor. Other doctors respected him, and he had a promising career ahead of him. But it was Kate's father who helped her make up her mind. He said, "Kate, don't marry a man unless you love everything about him. You've worked hard to achieve your **profession**, and you've been successful at it . . . but more than anything, I want you to be happy."

With those words ringing in her ears, Kate returned to Detroit and married the mechanic, Bill Newcomb.

Unlike Pat, Bill did not expect Kate to give up being a doctor. When Kate got called to deliver a baby on their wedding night, Bill cheerfully waited in the car for her. He continued to do this for Kate all through their marriage, driving her out to her late-night calls and keeping her company.

With Kate's skill and Bill's encouragement, Kate's practice blossomed. Soon Dr. Levy, a well-known **pediatrician**, asked Kate to join his practice. When she agreed, a party was thrown in her honor. Kate couldn't help but remember that

profession: a job that requires special education, such as law or medicine   **pediatrician** (pee dee uh **trish** uhn): a doctor who takes care of babies and children

fancy dinner with the squab years earlier. But this celebration was much different. Kate had come a long way from that night in Boston. Now she was clearly at the start of a bright and promising medical career.

No one knew it, but as they laughed and talked, a shadow was creeping into Bill and Kate's happy lives.

And it all started with just a little cough from Bill at the party.

3
The Northwoods

Bill's cough grew worse. Soon he was coming home from work pale and tired. Then he lost weight and didn't have the strength to go to work at all. Tests were done. The news was not good.

During World War I, Bill had worked in a **defense plant** where planes and tanks were built. No one knew that the air in these factories was harmful. None of the workers wore **protective** masks. The air Bill breathed was filled with tiny pieces of metal. The metal had stayed inside his lungs, and now his lungs weren't getting the oxygen he needed into his blood. Worst of all, there was no cure for his **condition**. The doctors told Kate and Bill that he would only get worse.

Bill couldn't stand to have Kate worry about him, but he simply could not remain in the city. He begged Kate to let

defense plant: a factory that builds weapons for war **protective**: made to keep someone safe from harm
condition: a medical problem that lasts for a long period of time

him return to the clean air of the northwoods that he had known growing up in Michigan. But Kate didn't want him to go. She was afraid he was leaving so that he could die. Still, she could not say no to his only wish. She agreed that he should first visit his family in Milwaukee. From there, he headed to the northern part of Wisconsin.

When Kate visited her husband a few weeks later, she was pleasantly surprised. Bill looked better. He didn't get tired as easily, and his skin wasn't as pale as before. Bill claimed that northern Wisconsin was good for him. He said that he was getting better.

This was very good news . . . but Kate missed Bill terribly. She faced a difficult decision. She had to choose between being a doctor and being with Bill. She couldn't have both. And so, despite all her **ambition**, all her training, and all her years of sacrifice, Dr. Kate told Dr. Levy that she was quitting. Tearfully, she said good-bye to her friends and fellow doctors. She would join Bill in the northwoods of Wisconsin.

ambition (am **bish** uhn): a strong desire to be successful

23

When she arrived by train at the tiny village of Eagle River, Kate probably felt as though she had stepped back in time. Eagle River was a far cry from the **bustling** city of Detroit. The village had very few phone lines, and even electricity was rare. When she arrived, the snow was so deep that the only way to get to their new home was by sleigh. Most roads were dirt or gravel and were not plowed during the winter.

Kate is ready to head to the northwoods of Wisconsin to join Bill, her husband.

Bill and Kate's 2-room log cabin was 18 miles from the nearest town—an all-day trip in winter. It was a very simple home. There was no electricity, no furnace, and no indoor plumbing. In the northwoods, snow fell early—in October, sometimes— and stayed on the ground until May. Kate had arrived in early January, when the snow was already waist-deep. But Bill told

bustling: full of movement and sound

her it would probably get even higher! In the northwoods, snow sometimes piled so high people had to tunnel out their windows just so they didn't **suffocate**. They had to dig ramps from their front doors *up* to the top of the snow to get in and out of their houses. During those long winters, people of the northern woods felt far away not just from the cities but from their neighbors as well. Luckily for Kate, she had Bill.

Northern Wisconsin was an isolated place—especially in winter, where snow made it nearly impossible to travel.

Surviving winter in the northwoods took effort. With Bill, Kate took part in the many tasks necessary for survival. She pulled a **crosscut saw** to cut logs for their **wood-burning stove**. She cleared heavy snow off their roof so it wouldn't collapse under the snow's weight. She also pulled water up

suffocate: to die from lack of oxygen   **crosscut saw**: a saw that can make cuts across the trunk of a tree
wood-burning stove: a stove that is fueled by wood, often used for both cooking and heating

25

from their well and scrubbed their laundry on a **washboard**. When spring came, she made syrup from the maple trees that surrounded the cabin. And in summe she wore **netting** to protect herself from the buzzing mosquitoes. Friends from Detroit and her father in Boston wrote her, begging her to return home. But as Bill's health grew stronger, her city life faded away. Kate found happiness in her simple life.

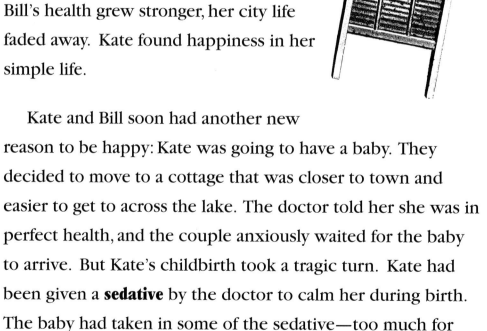

Kate and Bill soon had another new reason to be happy: Kate was going to have a baby. They decided to move to a cottage that was closer to town and easier to get to across the lake. The doctor told her she was in perfect health, and the couple anxiously waited for the baby to arrive. But Kate's childbirth took a tragic turn. Kate had been given a **sedative** by the doctor to calm her during birth. The baby had taken in some of the sedative—too much for his little body to handle. Just two days after he was born, her baby boy died.

washboard: a board with slats used to rub clothes against when washing by hand   **netting**: fabric that looks like a net, usually used as protection from insects   **sedative** (**sed** uh tiv): a drug that makes a person sleepy and relaxed

After **devoting** her life to helping mothers give birth to healthy babies, her own child's death seemed especially unfair. It was more than Kate could bear. She was numb, and she was bitter. It would be years before Kate would be able to endure the sight of a doctor, even, she said, "the one who looked back at me from my own mirror."

In the years that followed, Kate and Bill slowly recovered. They made themselves a home in the woods along Rice Creek. Bill earned money by hunting and guiding tourists around the lakes. And Kate came to value the community around her. The loggers, hunters, Ojibwe Indians, and people who vacationed there in the summer became their friends. Kate learned to follow a trail, to read the weather, to catch and fry fish, and to hunt. She even learned to snowshoe. Kate and Bill spent long winter hours listening to the radio and reading. The books they enjoyed were delivered to them by the "penny engine," a **logging train** that ran by their cabin. But during these long, quiet winters, one thing Kate never read about was medicine. She was certain she would never be a doctor again.

devoting: giving time, effort, and attention   **logging train**: train carrying wood that has been sawn into planks

In 1928, Kate and Bill had another child, Tommy, who learned to love the woods as much as they did. Tommy was the reason Kate finally met Dr. Torpy, the only doctor in the northwoods. She brought Tommy in to see the doctor after his fingers were crushed in a car door. When Dr. Torpy found out that Kate herself was a doctor, he was angry with her.

"Hmph!" exclaimed Dr. Torpy. "An expert doctor, **holed up** in the **backwoods** doing housework. It's a waste of talent."

Kate and Bill's second child, Tommy, was born at their cabin on Rice Creek in 1928.

Tommy loved to fish and hunt with his father.

holed up: hidden away   **backwoods**: an area of forest far from cities or towns

"I'm through with medicine," Kate told him, and left. Though she had done her best to ignore the doctor, his comments did get her thinking about it again.

Then one night, she got a phone call from Dr. Torpy. A woman was deathly ill with pneumonia just 8 miles from Kate's cabin. A blizzard raged outside, and Dr. Torpy was too far away to make it in time. Could Kate check on her? Kate said no. After all, she didn't have a **medical license**. Hers had **expired** years ago! Dr. Torpy insisted Kate help the sick woman.

The doctor shouted, "That woman will die if you don't get to her! And by the way, from now on, you're taking all the calls in your end of the county. Understand?"

Kate had no other choice but to go. After all, if Dr. Torpy couldn't help the woman, who else but Kate could? She brushed the dust off her medical bag, and Bill drove her to the woman's home. The snow was so deep that Kate and Bill had to stop the car and snowshoe the last 2 miles.

medical license: a certificate that says a person is allowed to practice medicine **expired**: to no longer be good or usable

29

When she finally got there, Kate made a **vaporizer** out of a tomato can and some wire. The vaporizer made it possible for the woman to breathe more easily. Kate's quick thinking had saved the woman's life.

After the storm ended, Kate paid a visit to Dr. Torpy. "I guess you'll have to take over my calls up my way..." she began. Dr. Torpy started to protest. Then Kate finished, "...until I get back from Madison. I'm going to take out my license."

Dr. Kate was back.

vaporizer (vayp ur ɪz ur): a machine that can change water or medicine into steam (or vapor) to make breathing easier

4

The Angel on Snowshoes

Before she knew it, Dr. Kate was back from Madison and swamped with patients. Doctors were few and far between in the northwoods. Dr. Torpy was serving a community almost 300 square miles—that's 3 times bigger than the area of Milwaukee!

Soon, Dr. Kate had a set of "offices" in town halls and schoolhouses throughout the area. She didn't have an office of her own. Besides, she spent most of her time on the road, making house calls. Because the roads were covered in either mud or snow, she visited her patients by car, boat, snowshoe, and even snowmobile—whatever it took. Most of the time Bill drove along with her, often with Tommy at his side. Sometimes, growing up, Tommy wished he had a "cookie mother instead of a doctor mother." But nothing stood between Kate and her patients.

Dr. Kate drove more than 100 miles and saw 20 to 45 patients each day. She set broken bones, soothed fevers, healed infections, stitched wounds, and performed surgeries.

Dr. Kate traveled to see her patients by car, by canoe, and even by snowmobile.

Most important to her was her work caring for **expectant** mothers. Over her career, she delivered almost 4,000 babies in the woods of northern Wisconsin. Not one of these mothers died under her care.

Dr. Kate knew every cabin, cottage, shack, and home on every back road. If someone needed a doctor but didn't have a phone, the family would tie a red rag to a branch along her route. When Kate saw it, she would stop in. Often,

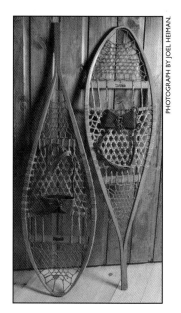

PHOTOGRAPH BY JOEL HEIMAN.

Dr. Kate kept a pair of snowshoes in her car just in case the snow became too deep for her to drive.

expectant (ek **spek** tent): pregnant, expecting a baby

32

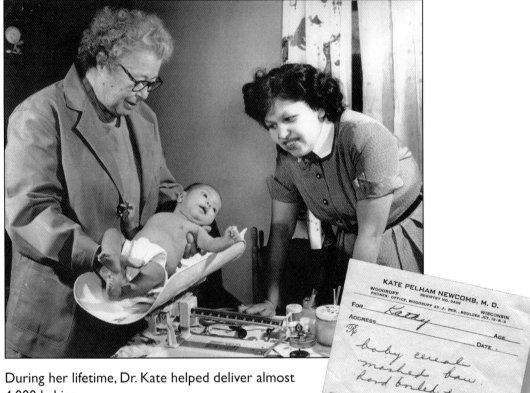

During her lifetime, Dr. Kate helped deliver almost 4,000 babies.

A prescription written out
by Dr. Kate for a new baby.

Kate was so busy she didn't have time to sleep. Once, she delivered 7 babies, traveled 376 miles, visited 3 different hospitals in 3 different cities, and made 17 house calls—all in under 36 hours!

The Great Depression and Northern Wisconsin

The Great Depression of the 1930s was a very difficult time in the United States. One out of every 4 workers did not have a job. Back then, the government did not help if a person could not find work. When a family could not afford to buy food, they simply starved. Many people lost their homes as well. In 1933, President Franklin Roosevelt began many new programs to help Americans during these hard times. The government created jobs and programs to get workers employed and families fed. Even so, getting out of the Depression was a tough battle.

Life in Wisconsin's northwoods was particularly hard. Many families had been **lured** to northern Wisconsin by the promise of cheap farmland. This promise was made good by the lumber industry. After the trees were cut down, the lumber companies no longer had any use for the land, so they sold it cheaply as farmland. Timberland did not necessarily make good soil for farming. Farmers who

WHI IMAGE ID 44582

During the Great Depression, much of the cheap farmland still had stumps left by lumber companies.

lured: led into a trap, tricked

bought this land found that while the trees had been cleared, tree stumps stayed behind—hundreds of stumps. Each stump took a day or more of expensive, backbreaking labor to pull up! Many families gave up. Those that did clear their land discovered that the growing season was so short that they could barely raise one crop. Families who stayed **eked** by.

One of the few ways people made a living in the northwoods was through summer **tourism**. **Resorts** and restaurants opened throughout northern Wisconsin. Many offered services such as **guided** fishing and hunting trips to the rich vacationers from Milwaukee and Chicago. But tourism made money only a few months out of the year. And if the weather was bad, business suffered. This is one reason why Dr. Kate's patients were rarely able to pay her in cash. Firewood and deer meat were much easier to find than dollar bills!

Money from tourism helped northwoods families survive during the Depression.

eked (eekd): survived on very little **tourism** (**tur** iz uhm): traveling and visiting places for pleasure **resort** (ree **zort**): a place where people go for rest and relaxation **guided**: led by an expert

35

Dr. Kate never sent a bill to her patients. Instead, she was paid in wood for her stove, vegetables for her dinner, and **venison** for her stew. In most cases, especially during the lean years of the **Great Depression**, this was all her patients could afford to pay. If pressed for an amount, she always answered, "Would $10 be all right?" That was pretty low pay for a doctor at the time, even in the northwoods. The local newspaper joked,

> *There's scarcely a family in these back woods*
> *Has any amount of **worldly good**,*
> *But Doc, she treats 'em all the same*
> *Keeps a-comin' till they're up again,*
> *And gets her pay, when not in cash,*
> *In green **cordwood** and garden trash.*

It's no wonder that Dr. Kate became known as the "Angel on Snowshoes."

---

venison (ven i sin): the meat from a deer   **Great Depression** (dee pre shuhn): a period during the 1930s when many people in America and other countries lost their jobs and homes   **worldly good**: riches or wealth   **cordwood**: wood that is cut and stacked in a pile

Dr. Kate worked in the morning; she worked at night. Her phone was always ringing. But taking care of her neighbors wasn't her only goal. She and Bill were also involved in building a school and a church for the community. And she was involved in other ways. In 1931, Dr. Kate was chosen to be the area's **health officer**. As health officer, it was her job to watch over the health of the community and stop disease from spreading. After taking the job, she received many calls from people who were sick due to **unsanitary** conditions. Dr. Kate took the problem seriously. She immediately had the lake waters tested. When bacteria from **sewage** was found in the water, she called the community together and taught people how to avoid polluting their water.

Next on her list was the milk supply. For a long time, there had been complaints about the milk's quality and purity. Dr. Kate sent samples to be tested at the State Health Laboratories in Madison, the state capital. When the results came back, she made a poster to put up around the community. On it, she listed which companies were doing a good job—and which were not. Soon, people started to buy

health officer: a person whose job it is to watch over a community's health and stop the spread of disease
unsanitary (un **san** i tair ree): not clean; full of germs **sewage** (**soo** ij): liquid and solid waste that is carried away in sewers and drains

milk only from the companies whose milk was safe. Kate did not make many friends with the other milk companies, but the quality of the milk got better. Dr. Kate's patients benefited from her ability to speak up.

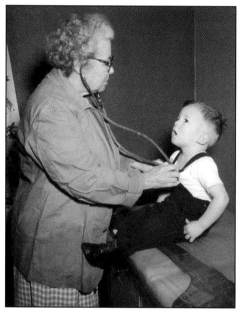

Dr. Kate helped thousands of kids like this one grow up to be healthy and strong.

Because she had been an excellent health officer, Dr. Kate was asked to make sure the local summer camps were healthy places for the kids who attended. Back then, there were no rules for the health of the campers. Dr. Kate took charge. Right away, she checked the quality of the water in each camp to make sure it was safe to drink. She examined the kitchens to see that they were clean, and she made sure camps had infirmaries where campers could go if they became ill or got hurt. She also insisted the children be **vaccinated** against

vaccinated (**vak** si nay ted): given a shot or pill to protect against disease

diseases such as **tetanus**. At Dr. Kate's urging, every child had a physical exam before attending camp. Dr. Kate's **guidelines** were so complete that the American Camping Association and the American Association of Pediatrics began to use them in camps across the nation.

Summer campers lined up for their checkups from Dr. Kate.

tetanus (**tet** nis): an infection in a cut that causes muscles to become stiff and can lead to death
guideline: a rule about how something should be done

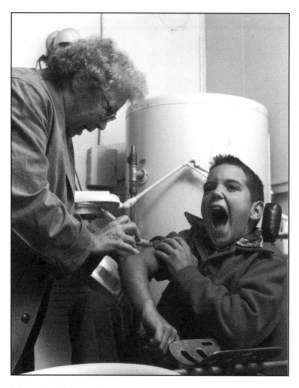

Not all of Dr. Kate's patients enjoyed seeing her!

Dr. Kate's busy life flew by. In 1936, Kate and Bill adopted a sister for Tommy from the State Home for Children. Her name was Eldorah. When they adopted her, Eldorah was **malnourished**. Her leg had been injured and had not healed properly, and she had a limp. Dr. Kate was there to nurse her daughter back to health, a job she did with pleasure. The little girl fit in perfectly with her new family and brought them much joy.

And there were more changes. In 1942, Dr. Kate got a permanent office, a small house made of logs in the town of Woodruff. The glassed-in front porch served as a waiting

malnourished (mal **nur** ishd): not having enough food, or not eating the right kinds of food to be healthy

40

room, while the kitchen and pantry were turned into **examining rooms**—mothers to the left, children to the right. Medical supplies were kept in the kitchen cabinets. At the back of the house was a small bedroom where Dr. Kate stayed when the roads were too bad to travel.

In the waiting room of her new office, Kate hung a picture with these words. It stayed up for as long as she was a doctor:

I expect to go through this life but once.
Any good, therefore, that I can do,
or any kindness that I can show my
fellow-man, let me do it now.
Let me not ***defer*** *nor neglect it,*
for I shall not pass this way again.

Dr. Kate wore her coat and **stethoscope** when working in her office.

---

examining room: a room in a doctor's office where the doctor meets with patients   **defer** (dee **fur**): to put someing off until later   **stethoscope** (**ste** thuhs kohp): a medical instrument used by doctors and nurses to listen to the heart, lungs, and other areas

PHOTOGRAPH BY JOEL HEIMAN, DISPLAY COURTESY OF THE DR. KATE PELHAM NEWCOMB MUSEUM.

Here is some of the equipment, tools, and medicines that Dr. Kate carried in her medical bag when she visited patients.

While her new office made it easier for Kate to see her patients, she still kept long hours and drove many miles each day. The nearest hospital was in Tomahawk—a drive that could take hours when the weather was bad. Dr. Kate desperately wanted a hospital to be built close by.

In 1949, Dr. Kate saved the life of Mrs. Arthur Rubloff, a wealthy woman visiting from Chicago. The woman's husband, Mr. Rubloff, asked Kate if there was anything she needed—

some way he could show his thanks to her. Kate answered, "The only thing I really want is a hospital, and that's like asking for the moon. But you can see for yourself how badly we need a hospital around here, and even a small one would be better than none."

Mr. Rubloff took her seriously. The next day, he **donated** $1,000 of his own money toward making a hospital for Dr. Kate. Soon a **board of directors** was created. It was made up of people who lived in the northwoods. They met together to decide how to raise **funds** for the hospital and to figure out what they needed. Hope grew in Dr. Kate and her patients.

Just how much money would a hospital cost? The board of directors came back with discouraging news. In order to build the hospital, Dr. Kate needed $110,000. That's a lot of money, even today. They would have to find people to donate money to the project. For a community that paid its doctor's bills with firewood and vegetables, the task seemed impossible. But Dr. Kate and her new board of directors were not about to give up!

donated: gave **board of directors**: group of people chosen to make decisions for a company, hospital, or school **funds**: money collected or set aside for a special purpose

5

The Million Penny Parade

Three years after that amazing first donation, the community had raised only half of the money they needed for the hospital. Still, the board felt it was time to start building. On July 3, 1952, construction began. Three 4-leaf clovers were found in the first shovelful of earth—a promising beginning! Despite this lucky start, funds for the hospital grew slowly. There just wasn't enough money to cover the cost of building. Plus, the hospital still needed money to pay the staff, buy medical equipment, and keep the building in good shape.

Construction began on the Lakeland Memorial Hospital in July of 1952.

Construction moved slowly. It was hard for Dr. Kate not to be disappointed.

Little did she know a surprise was just around the corner. The Arbor Vitae-Woodruff High School stood just a few blocks from the construction site. Built in 1941, its students came from all over the area. The class of 1953 was its largest so far—22 **seniors** would **graduate** that spring. Dr. Kate had been at the birth of almost every one of them! As they began their senior year, something happened that really got the hospital construction moving.

It all started with a clever lesson by the school's geometry teacher, Otto Burich. On a bright fall afternoon in 1952, Mr. Burich asked his class to close their eyes and imagine a million of something. What would it look like? How much space would it take up? The class counted the holes in the ceiling tiles and **calculated** how many **square feet** it would take to reach a million. But that wasn't very exciting. Then they talked about collecting a million of something, just so they could see the pile. What would a million acorns look like? What about a million stones? Then one girl said she'd like to see a million

senior (**seen** yur): a student in the final year of high school graduate (**graj** oo ayt): to finish school
calculated (**kal** kyoo lay ted): worked out by using arithmetic square foot: an area 12 inches long and 12 inches wide

45

pennies all together. The rest of the class liked the idea. A million pennies. Imagine. That's $10,000! But what would they do with it?

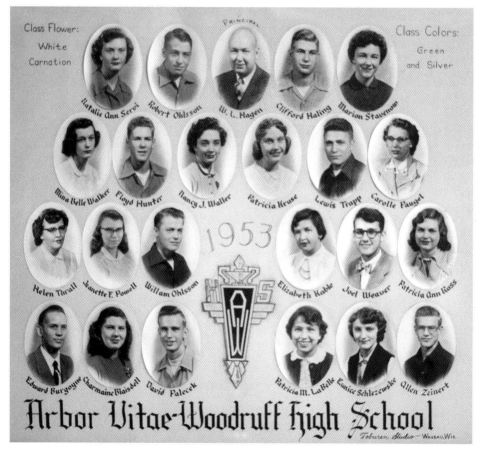

Class Flower:
White
Carnation

PRINCIPAL

Class Colors:
Green
and Silver

Natalie Ann Serot   Robert Ohlsson   W. L. Hagen   Clifford Haling   Marion Stavenau

Mina Belle Walker   Floyd Hunter   Nancy J. Waller   Patricia Kruse   Lewis Trapp   Carolle Paugel

Helen Thrall   Jeanette F. Powell   William Ohlsson   Elizabeth Kable   Joel Weaver   Patricia Ann Ross

Edward Burgoyne   Charmaine Blaisdell   David Palecek   Patricia M. LaBelle   Eunice Schlezewske   Allen Zeinert

1953

Toburen Studio — Wausau, Wis.

Arbor Vitae-Woodruff High School

The Arbor Vitae–Woodruff High School class of 1953 had 22 students—its largest yet.

That's when the class thought of Dr. Kate's hospital just up the road. Construction had stopped when the hospital ran out of funds. What if they gave the pennies to the hospital? Suddenly, everyone was excited. The "Million Penny Paraders" were born.

The Million Penny Parade soon took over the whole school. Everyone wanted to take part in the **campaign** to collect one million pennies. After Otto's class had donated their own pennies, they asked the school's typing students for help. In the 1950s, there were no copy machines or printers. Letters asking for donations had to be typed one by one. The students rolled 500 pieces of paper into the school's typewriters and typed 500 letters for the campaign. The letters explained what the students were trying to do and asked for donations. These letters were sent to members of the community as well as to people who spent summers in the area.

campaign (kam **payn**): an organized effort over time to achieve a certain goal

Original Letter of the Penny Parade

Have you ever seen a MILLION — a MILLION of anything? Few people have. During a class discussion concerning numbers and amounts, the students in the GEOMETRY class of the Arbor Vitae-Woodruff High School expressed their desire to see, if possible, a MILLION pennies.

Thus came into existence the promotion of a program to collect 1,000,000 pennies. It is realized that this program is indeed a task that will require considerable effort on the part of every individual assisting in this promotion. However, with assistance and cooperation from everyone, this goal will be attained.

OTTO F. BURICH
Geometry Teacher

Every department in the AV-W High School is cooperating in this project. Consider the learning aspects of this project wherein the ENGLISH Department is assisting in composition, the HISTORY Classes in monetary background, the SCIENCE Department in coinage, the COMMERCIAL Department in typing, bookkeeping, and banking, the MUSIC Department in entertainment, the INDUSTRIAL ARTS Department in construction and publicity and the MATHEMATICS Department as the nucleus, in counting and operations.

In order to keep expenses of promotion at a minimum, this letter is published by the commercial department. All other exepnses will be handled and all work done by the Mathematics department.

This project has the sanction of the Arbor Vitae-Woodruff Board of Education and the Board of the Lakeland Memorial Hospital.

In launching a program such as this, the STUDENTS PROMOTERS were very much aware of the dire need for a hospital in an area such as Woodruff, Wisconsin. Thus, these same students decided that, after their goal was accomplished the amount contained therein would be donated as a sum to Lakeland Memorial Hospital now under construction. This program is twofold, first as a learning project, and second as a practical accomplishment to help complete a very necessary structure.

This plea is most humbly extended for your cooperation in the form of a donation. Please JOIN this 1,000,000 PENNY PARADE — NOW!

It is desired to accomplish this huge task as expeditiously and with as little expense as possible. If you do not find it convenient to send your pennies, your gratuity will be accepted in any form and transferred into PENNIES by the PARADE promoters.

An accurate record will, of necessity, be kept. Any donor of 100 pennies or more, or the equivalent, will be listed in the BIG 1,000,000 PENNY PARADE BOOK.

In order to keep expenses down to a minimum, a post card of acknowledgement will be sent unless a receipt is requested with a self-addressed stamped envelope. However, the PARADE BOOK will be open to inspection at the time the PENNIES are on exhibition.

Join the BIG PARADE NOW! Forward your pennies or donations to:

The 1,000,000 PENNY PARADE, AV—W High School, Woodruff, Wisconsin

and—THANKS A MILLION

Very gratefully,

THE MILLION PENNY PARADERS

A copy of the letter that the Million Penny Paraders typed and mailed.

The pennies started rolling in. As they arrived, the math class created graphs to keep track of penny totals. The social studies class made a map to show where the pennies came from. Each person who donated a dollar or more had his or her name written down in the "penny book." A group of students sent thank-you cards to donors.

And the pennies started pouring in!

Social studies students mapped the locations of where every donation came from.

The energy of the high school students was **contagious**.

contagious (kuhn **tay** jis): catching

Everyone in Woodruff seemed to have caught the spirit of the Penny Parade. Area businesses put out jars for people to drop their pennies into. Churches held raffles and hosted pancake dinners. Money from dances, basketball games, and even a talent show all went to the hospital fund. People who had once paid Dr. Kate in firewood, chickens, and fresh vegetables dug deep in their pockets to give their spare change. And pennies weren't the only things donated. People offered cement, wood, building supplies, and **labor**. But would it be enough to finish the hospital?

By Christmas, the Penny Paraders were a quarter of the way to one million pennies. Their success was gaining attention.

The penny campaign got attention from across the country. This cartoon was in the popular *Look* magazine.

City newspapers from as far away as Milwaukee and Chicago ran stories about the penny campaign. Then the national news picked

labor: physical work

up the story. Suddenly, the Million Penny Parade for Dr. Kate's hospital was played on **newsreels** across America.

Otto Burich, the teacher whose class came up with the idea for the Million Penny Parade, counts pennies.

So many donations were made that the students had to carry heavy buckets of pennies to the bank every day. The students continued to graph their progress, map the places donations came from, and write thank-you notes. What had started out as a small geometry class project quickly became a **mission** for all of America. Everyone wanted to help make Dr. Kate's dream for a northwoods hospital come true.

It wasn't just pennies that started arriving in Woodruff. Some donors sent letters, too. "I'll never forget the long ride to Tomahawk with a broken leg last summer," wrote one man who sent in his spare change. Another letter came with a handful of pennies all the way from Korea, where the United States was in the middle of a war. "I read about your campaign to collect enough pennies to build the new hospital in your community,"

newsreel: a short film of recent news that played before a movie in a theater started in the 1940s and 1950s
mission (**mi** shuhn): a special purpose or task

51

wrote Corporal G. E. Whitmore. "I hope these will in a small way help your goal. We have no use for pennies here, and I have had these sixteen months since I arrived here." A fourth-grade teacher from Hill School in **Thormopolis**, Wyoming, wrote, "It has been called to my attention that Wyoming hasn't contributed to your Penny Parade. Our fourth grade is **enclosing** a dollar from their **club** money to the Penny Parade. Hope you receive many more dollars from Wyoming."

Donations arrived from all around the country and the world.

Soon the high schoolers from Woodruff had received donations from every state in the country and 23 **foreign** countries. More than 60,000 people sent money for the hospital that year! Many people donated more than just pennies. Some sent nickels and quarters. Others sent crumpled dollar bills or wrote checks. By the middle of April,

Thormopolis (thur **mop** oh lis)   **enclosing**: putting inside an envelope   **club**: a group of students who meet to share a common interest

104 school days after they started, the Million Penny Paraders had raised $10,000.

Still, they hadn't *exactly* reached their original goal of seeing what a million of something would look like. Not all of the money they received was in pennies. And with so many trips to the bank, no one had seen all of the pennies at once. So the Million Penny Paraders started planning a celebration. It would take place on Memorial Day, the last Saturday in May. By that time, school would be nearly over for the year and vacationers would be arriving for the summer.

On May 30, the celebration began. Townspeople and tourists filled the sidewalks to watch as the parade streamed by, complete with marching bands and colorful **floats**. At the head of the parade, the "Penny Queen," high schooler Donna Behn, waved to the crowd. She had been chosen by her classmates to lead the parade. And the best part of the Penny Parade? In the gym of the high school, for everyone to see, was a huge pile of pennies: one million to be exact.

foreign (for uhn)   **float**: at a parade, a decorated truck or platform

Thousands of people came to see the Million Penny Parade on Memorial Day in 1953.

The penny queen, Donna Behn, up to her waist in one million pennies.

Before the parade, **armored trucks** from banks in Milwaukee and Minneapolis had driven into town, each filled with pennies. These were dumped on the floor of the gym. Everyone was amazed when they saw the pile: 20 feet long and 26 feet wide. It was huge. And it was about to get larger.

For days and weeks after the parade, visitors still flocked to the high school in Woodruff to see the million penny pile. That summer, while the **Wisconsin National Guard** watched over the coins, 56,000 people from all over the world streamed in to see the pennies. Kids played in them. People tried to lift heavy shovelfuls. Visitors bought penny earrings, signed the penny

armored (**ahr** murd) **truck:** a truck with a thick metal covering, used to carry money or valuable items
Wisconsin National Guard: soldiers who volunteer to serve the state of Wisconsin

book, and had their pictures taken in the sea of pennies. They collected Dr. Kate **seals**, special stamps printed with a picture of Dr. Kate. Most of the visitors added their own pennies to the pile before they left.

By the end of that summer, the Million Penny Paraders had been more successful than anyone had ever dreamed. They had done it, and more. When the pennies were counted, they had almost doubled in number; 1.7 million pennies—$17,000— shone on the floor of the school gymnasium.

The Penny Parade achieved the students' goal, and the building of the hospital was finally able to move forward. But there were more costs. Equipment was still very expensive. And they still needed to hire staff and order supplies. That following year, Dr. Kate found that some of her cases still had to be sent to the hospital in Tomahawk.

Dr. Kate was tickled that the students—many of whom she delivered as babies—took part in the penny drive.

seals: stamps with a special design

55

A Million Pennies

At the parade and all through the summer of 1953, The Million Penny Paraders handed visitors a pamphlet that explained what the penny campaign was for. Inside, they listed some penny **statistics**.

- Piled in a single column the one million pennies will make a column 5,000 feet high.
- Placed side by side, the pennies would produce a ribbon of copper 11.84 miles long.
- If 10 pennies weigh 1.107 ounces, one million of them will weigh 6918.75 pounds or 3.459 tons.
- One million pennies placed side by side will cover an area of 3906.24 square feet.
- A 2-yard dump truck would not be able to haul one million pennies all at once.

And here are some penny facts from today:

- Pennies were the very first coins to be **minted** in the United States in 1787.
- Benjamin Franklin designed the first pennies.
- The U.S. Mint produces more than 13 billion pennies each year; that's more than 30 million a day.
- Pennies are expected to last 25 years.

statistic (stuh **tis** tik): a fact or piece of information presented in numbers   **minted**: made into money

6

This Is Your Life!

By 1954, news of the Million Penny Parade had reached
Hollywood. One of Dr. Kate's patients contacted Ralph
Edwards, a television star and the **host** of the popular program
This Is Your Life. During each show, Ralph asked someone
from the audience to come up onstage. No one knew ahead
of time who would be chosen. Sometimes, it was somebody
famous, such as a movie star or popular singer. Other times, it
was an ordinary person—someone who never guessed his or
her name might be called.

After the **featured guest** made it onstage, family and friends
who had been hiding behind the stage came forward. One
by one, they would each tell a story from the guest's life. The
audience could see them, but the guest could not. As each
story was finished, Ralph would ask if his guest recognized

---

host: the person in charge of a television program who talks with celebrities and other guests
featured (fee churd) **guest**: the main guest on a television program

the voice from the past. When Ralph Edwards heard Dr. Kate's story, he wanted her to be a guest on his show.

While being chosen for the program was always a surprise to the featured guest, much planning had to be done ahead of time to pull it off. For one thing, how could they get Dr. Kate to travel all the way to California from Wisconsin? They had to come up with an excuse. The **producers** of the show figured that Dr. Kate probably wouldn't visit California just to take a vacation. But maybe she would visit if it would help people back home in the northwoods. The show teamed up with the Los Angeles County Medical Society and the Wisconsin Medical Association. They invited Kate to attend a medical **conference** in Los Angeles. They even said they would pay for her to come. But Kate wasn't sure she should go. Didn't her patients need her? And what about the hospital? It was almost complete.

Kate's friends and family insisted, and after much **prodding**, Kate finally accepted the offer. It was the first time she had been out of the state of Wisconsin in years. As she packed her bags to leave, probably the last thing she suspected was that she was about to become a television star.

producer: a person in charge of putting on a play or making a movie or television program   **conference**: a large meeting where people in the same profession get together to discuss ideas and opinions
prodding: encouragement or urging

On March 17, 1954, Dr. Kate sat in the audience of *This Is Your Life*, restless. She hadn't wanted to go to the show at all! Her friends had had to talk her into it. Then the host, Ralph Edwards, started asking people in the audience where they were from. He even asked Dr. Kate, who wished he would move on to someone else. Suddenly, a spotlight shone on her. "Dr. Kate Pelham Newcomb, this is your life!" shouted Ralph. A **bewildered** Dr. Kate stumbled up to the stage. She wasn't quite sure what was going on. Not only did she think she was in Los Angeles for a meeting, but she hardly ever watched television. The one television station available in Woodruff was often full of static. And Woodruff didn't get NBC, the station that broadcast Ralph Edwards's show. In fact, before that day, Dr. Kate had never even heard of *This Is Your Life*! She had no idea what to expect.

Dr. Kate with *This Is Your Life* television host, Ralph Edwards.

"I don't know what's going on," she kept **murmuring** as Ralph

bewildered (bee **wil** durd): very confused   **murmuring**: speaking very quietly

59

Edwards brought up things about her life. Dr. Kate had no idea how he knew these things! Had he read them in one of the articles about the Penny Parade? The audience loved it.

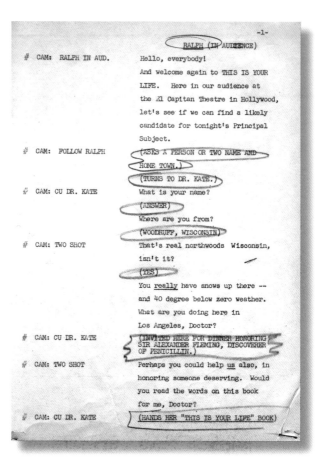

This is the script from Dr. Kate's appearance on *This Is Your Life*.

Then, one by one, her family, friends, and neighbors started telling stories. Her sister talked about Dr. Kate's childhood. Friends from Buffalo talked about her life during medical school. Her son Tommy told the story of how Dr. Torpy had gotten her to start working as a doctor again. Old friends and neighbors talked about Dr. Kate's near-death experiences in the cold and how many lives she had saved back in Wisconsin. Each time a new story was told, Kate had to guess who was telling it.

"You stinkers," Dr. Kate said, as she began to see how many people had secretly worked together to get her on the TV show. The audience roared with laughter.

Then Otto Burich, the geometry teacher from Woodruff, came out. One of the Million Penny Paraders, Eva May Clausen, was with him. They talked about the campaign to raise money for the hospital and the Million Penny Parade. And at the end of the program, Ralph Edwards turned to the audience to ask them if they had any pennies they could send

After Dr. Kate appeared on television, 400,000 people sent letters—and money.

Dr. Kate's way. He told them to mark their envelopes with "Dr. Kate, Woodruff, Wisconsin."

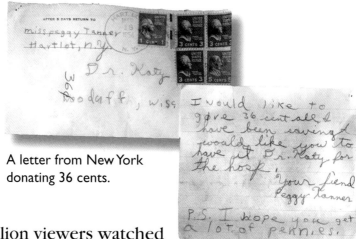

A letter from New York donating 36 cents.

About 40 million viewers watched the television program that night. And when the program ended, children, parents, doctors, lawyers, young and old, poor and rich, sent their pennies to Dr. Kate and her hospital.

That Saturday, Dr. Kate arrived home from California in her new red Mercury—a present given to her from Ralph Edwards and the producers of the show. Much to her surprise and amazement, there were already 80 mailbags of letters waiting for her in the tiny post office. Eighty mailbags full of letters, checks, dollar bills, coins, and pennies for the hospital!

Just like the pennies for the parade, the mailbags were hauled to the high school gym where people from the community lined up at tables to open the letters and count the money. Every bag, bucket, box, wastepaper basket, and bowl that could be found was used to help hold the coins. Excitement filled the air. Everyone

Dr. Kate with some of the mail that was waiting for her when she returned to Woodruff.

Hospital construction continues.

was hopeful that the hospital would finally get the money it needed!

Despite the enthusiasm in the high school, Dr. Kate slipped away. A patient needed her. The Lakeland Memorial Hospital wasn't open yet, so Dr. Kate made the long drive to the hospital in Tomahawk. Later on that night, she delivered a new baby. It was a little girl. Her parents named her Penny.

As the weeks went by, the letters continued to flood in. Four tons of mail—as heavy as an elephant—arrived addressed to Dr. Kate. There were a total of 176 mailbags. Each carried about $500 of donations. All in all, 400,000

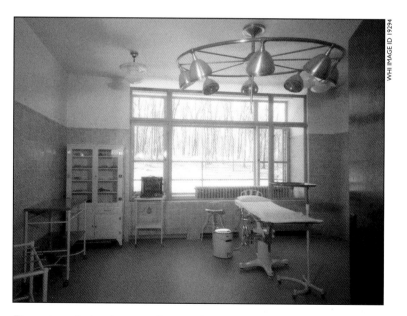

WHI IMAGE ID 19294

Donations helped to pay for modern operating rooms such as this one.

people wrote to Dr. Kate. They sent an amazing amount of money for the hospital: $110,000. That's 11 million more pennies!

The Lakeland Memorial Hospital opened in April 1954, with Dr. Kate as its chief of staff.

Soon, the hospital was able to pay for equipment and supplies, and it was staffed in the way Dr. Kate had always dreamed it might be. In April, the Lakeland Memorial Hospital opened its doors for the first time. It came as no surprise when Dr. Kate was named **chief of staff**.

For Memorial Day in 1954, just a year after the first parade, the town decided to have a second Million Penny Parade. This time even more people crammed the streets; 25,000 visitors craned their necks to watch as 90 floats and 15 marching bands went by. That day, the world's largest penny

chief of staff: the leader of all the hospital's workers

was **unveiled** in front of the high school. It had been put up in honor of the students of Arbor Vitae-Woodruff High School who had worked tirelessly on the penny campaign. This penny was 15 feet high and weighed more than 17,000 pounds. On

its front was stamped a date: 1953. More than 50 years later, you can still see the penny. It stands on the site where the high school used to be.

On July 21, 1954, the hospital was **dedicated** in a special **ceremony**. Dr. Kate was the guest of honor. The governor of the state of Wisconsin, Walter

On Memorial Day in 1954, at the second Million Penny Parade, the world's largest penny was unveiled.

unveiled (uhn **vayld**): uncovered, revealed   **dedicated**: to show thanks or appreciation
ceremony (**ser** uh moh nee): a formal event to mark an important occasion

Kohler, arrived by plane to speak at the ceremony. Inside the hospital, framed on the wall, were copies of the pages from the penny book—the list of every person who had donated more than a dollar for Dr. Kate's hospital.

After the governor's speech, the celebration shifted to the high school. But again, Dr. Kate missed out on the events. While the governor tossed his own coins onto the pile of pennies on the high school gym floor, Dr. Kate was on her way back to the hospital. Someone had almost drowned in the lake. Nothing stood in her way when someone needed her help.

This time Dr. Kate had a much shorter drive: to her own hospital, Lakeland Memorial.

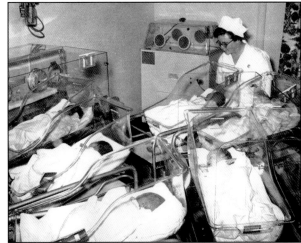

Finally, Dr. Kate and the new mothers had a hospital with a nursery for their newborn babies.

67

7
Remembering Dr. Kate

One of the people watching Dr. Kate on *This Is Your Life* was a Hollywood screenwriter named **Adele Comandini**. She was so taken with the story that she decided to write a book about Dr. Kate. Adele spent a great deal of time asking

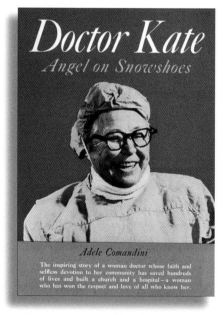

The cover of Dr. Kate's biography.

questions of Kate, her family, and her friends. She wanted to be sure she had all of the details of the story right. In 1956, Dr. Kate's biography, *Doctor Kate: Angel on Snowshoes*, was published. It became a national **bestseller**.

Sadly, Dr. Kate was not able to enjoy the success of the book or of the hospital for long. On May 30, 1956, the northwoods got

Adele Commandini (uh **del** coh muhn **dee** nee)   **bestseller**: a book that sells a very large number of copies

a late-season snowstorm. That night, on her way home from a meeting, Dr. Kate slipped on the icy steps of the Lac du Flambeau School. The fall broke her hip. The break was so serious that the ambulance took her not to her own hospital but to a larger one in Wausau. There, surgeons operated to fix the break, but she died during the surgery. The doctors claimed her heart was just too tired. The community thought it was probably because Dr. Kate had given all of it to her patients and her work.

Even though Dr. Kate is gone, her **legacy** lives on. It is estimated that Dr. Kate delivered close to 4,000 babies over her career. These people live

The hospital still stands today as the Dr. Kate Newcomb Convalescent Center.

all over the United States now, raising families of their own. And her hospital, the Lakeland Memorial? It's still there, an important part of the Woodruff community. In 1977, the hospital was

legacy (leg uh see): what someone leaves behind for the future generations after they have died

69

renamed the Dr. Kate Newcomb **Convalescent** Center. Patients with serious illnesses and injuries stayed there while they **recovered**. Later, the hospital became a **nursing home**, part of a larger hospital named the Howard Young Medical Center.

People still remember Dr. Kate, too. The high school is gone now, but the world's largest penny still towers tall as tourists snap their pictures next to it. And in 1988, the Dr. Kate Museum opened in the spot where her Woodruff office once stood. Inside, visitors giggle at Kate's bewilderment as they watch her on *This Is Your Life*. They marvel at the weight of her doctor bag and smile at the wall of photos of the babies she delivered. They imagine her trudging through the snow to her patients in the pair of snowshoes that hang on the wall.

In 2003, it had been 50 years since the first Million Penny Parade. The community decided to celebrate in the very best way: with a parade. Hundreds of Dr. Kate babies, now adults, returned to march down Main Street. But the part that Dr. Kate probably would have loved the most was how the local children got involved. Schools in the area held penny wars, each trying to collect more pennies than the rest. In the end,

convalescent (cahn vuh **les** ent): a person recovering from illness or injury   **recovered**: got better after illness or injury   **nursing home**: a place for the care of the very old or of anyone who needs nursing care over a long period of time

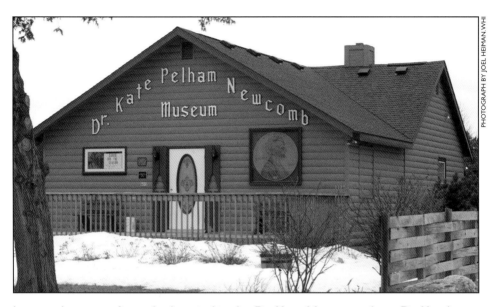

Just up the street from the hospital is the Dr. Kate Museum, where Dr. Kate's story lives on.

In 2003, on the fiftieth anniversary of the first Penny Parade, another penny campaign was held.

they collected $17,000, or 1.7 million pennies—the same amount as the original Million Penny Paraders! This money has been set aside for college **scholarships** for high school students who are going on to study medicine or education, Dr. Kate's two careers.

scholarship (**sko** lur ship): money given to help a student continue his or her schooling

And when they run out of the scholarship funds in the future?

Most likely, there'll be another penny drive, keeping the memory of Dr. Kate alive for a new generation.

Appendix

Dr. Kate's Time Line

1885
or 1886 — Kate Pelham is born on July 26 in Leoti, Kansas, to Kate and Tom Pelham.

1888 — Kate's mother and baby brother die in childbirth. Kate's father marries Nona Fenton.

1893 — The Pelhams move to Buffalo, New York.

1902 — Kate becomes engaged to her high school sweetheart, Robert.

1904 — Kate's fiance, Robert, dies of pneumonia. Kate graduates from high school in Buffalo, New York.

1905 — Kate finishes teacher training in Buffalo.

1906 — Kate teaches fifth and sixth grade at Public School 54 in Buffalo.

1907 — Kate's father, stepmother, and half-brothers and sisters move to Boston. Not long afterward, her stepmother dies and Kate moves to Boston.

1913 — Kate starts medical school at the University of Buffalo, New York.

1917 — Kate turns down a marriage proposal, graduates from medical school, and takes an internship in New York City, followed by one in Detroit.

1920 — Kate starts a medical practice in Detroit with three other women doctors.

1921 — Kate marries Bill Newcomb.

1922 — In early January, Kate gives up her practice and moves to northern Wisconsin.

1922 — Kate and Bill's first child dies in the autumn.

1928 — On January 29, Kate and Bill have a son, William Thomas Newcomb, or "Tommy."

1931 — Kate travels to Madison to get her Wisconsin medical license. She starts to practice medicine again. Kate is named the health officer of the community.

1936 — In March, Kate and Bill adopt a little girl, Eldorah.

1942 — Kate opens her office in Woodruff.

1949 — The hospital building fund is started. Construction begins in July.

1952 — The Million Penny Paraders start their campaign in November.

1953 — On May 30, the Million Penny Parade is held; 1.7 million pennies are collected in total.

1954 — On March 17, Dr. Kate is a guest on *This Is Your Life*.

1954 — On April 6, Kate delivers the first baby in the Lakeland Memorial Hospital.

1954 — The second Million Penny Parade is held in May, and the World's Largest Penny is unveiled.

1954 — Lakeland Memorial Hospital is dedicated on July 21.

1955 — The third Million Penny Parade is held.

1956 — Adele Comandini publishes *Doctor Kate: Angel on Snowshoes*.

1956 — On May 30, Dr. Kate dies in surgeryto repair her broken hip.

1972 — Lakeland Memorial Hospital changes its name to the Howard Young Medical Center.

1980 — The old hospital becomes the Dr. Kate Newcomb Convalescent Center.

2003 — In May, a Penny Parade is held in honor of the first parade, 50 years earlier.

Glossary

Pronunciation Key

a   c<u>a</u>t (kat), pl<u>ai</u>d (plad), h<u>a</u>lf (haf)

ah   f<u>a</u>ther (**fah** THur), h<u>ea</u>rt (hahrt)

air   c<u>a</u>rry (**kair** ee), b<u>ear</u> (bair), wh<u>ere</u> (whair)

aw   <u>a</u>ll (awl), l<u>aw</u> (law), b<u>ough</u>t (bawt)

ay   s<u>ay</u> (say), br<u>ea</u>k (brayk), v<u>ei</u>n (vayn)

e   b<u>e</u>t (bet), s<u>ay</u>s (sez), d<u>ea</u>f (def)

ee   b<u>ee</u> (bee), t<u>ea</u>m (teem), f<u>ea</u>r (feer)

i   b<u>i</u>t (bit), w<u>o</u>men (**wim** uhn), b<u>ui</u>ld (bild)

ɪ   <u>i</u>ce (ɪs), l<u>ie</u> (lɪ), sk<u>y</u> (skɪ)

o   h<u>o</u>t (hot), w<u>a</u>tch (wotch)

oh   <u>o</u>pen (**oh** puhn), s<u>ew</u> (soh)

oi   b<u>oi</u>l (boil), b<u>oy</u> (boi)

oo   p<u>oo</u>l (pool), m<u>o</u>ve (moov), sh<u>oe</u> (shoo)

or   <u>or</u>der (**or** dur), m<u>ore</u> (mor)

ou   h<u>ou</u>se (hous), n<u>ow</u> (nou)

u   g<u>oo</u>d (gud), sh<u>oul</u>d (shud)

uh   c<u>u</u>p (kuhp), fl<u>oo</u>d (fluhd), butt<u>o</u>n (**buht** uhn)

ur   b<u>ur</u>n (burn), p<u>ear</u>l (purl), b<u>ir</u>d (burd)

yoo   <u>u</u>se (yooz), f<u>ew</u> (fyoo), v<u>iew</u> (vyoo)

hw   <u>wh</u>at (hwuht), <u>wh</u>en (hwen)

TH   <u>th</u>at (THat), brea<u>the</u> (breeTH)

zh   mea<u>s</u>ure (**mezh** ur), gara<u>ge</u> (guh **razh**)

accept (ak **sept**): to agree to let someone attend a school or start a job

ambition (am **bish** uhn): a strong desire to be successful

applied: asked to be allowed to attend a school or work at a job

armored (**ahr** murd) **truck**: a truck with a thick metal covering, used to carry money or valuable items

backwoods: an area of forest far from cities or towns

bestseller: a book that sells a very large number of copies

bewildered (bee **wil** durd): very confused

board of directors: group of people chosen to make decisions for a company, hospital, or school

bustling: full of movement and sound

calculated (**kal** kyoo lay ted): worked out by using arithmetic

campaign (kam **payn**): an organized effort over time to achieve a certain goal

career: a profession

ceremony (**ser** uh moh nee): a formal event to mark an important occasion

chief of staff: the leader of all the hospital's workers

city hall: a public building used for government offices

club: a group of students who meet to share a common interest

compassion (kuhm **pash** uhn): a strong desire to help someone in need

condition: a medical problem that lasts for a long period of time

conference: a large meeting where people in the same profession get together to discuss ideas and opinions

contagious (kuhn **tay** jis): catching

convalescent (cahn vuh **les** ent): a person recovering from illness or injury

cordwood: wood that is cut and stacked in a pile

corset (**kor** sit): a close-fitting garment worn under the clothes to support and shape the waist, hips, and breasts

crosscut saw: a saw that can make cuts across the trunk of a tree

dedicated: to show thanks or appreciation

defense plant: a factory that builds weapons for war

defer (dee **fur**): to put off until later

devastated (**dev** uh stay tud): very upset, shocked

devoting: giving time, effort, and attention

donated: gave

duplicate (**doop** li kit): an exact copy of something, a double

eked (eekd): survived on very little

enclosing: putting inside an envelope

engaged: promised to marry

examining room: a room in a doctor's office where the doctor meets with patients

expectant (ek **spek** tent): pregnant, expecting a baby

expired: to no longer good or usable

featured (**fee** churd) **guest**: the main guest on a television program

float: at a parade, a decorated truck or platform

frostbitten: damaged by extreme cold

funds: money collected or set aside for a special purpose

graduate (**graj** oo ayt): to finish school

Great Depression (dee **pre** shuhn): a period during the 1930s when many people in America and other countries lost their jobs and homes

guided: led by an expert

guideline: a rule about how something should be done

gusto (**guhs** toh): joy or enthusiasm

health officer: a person whose job it is to watch over a community's health and stop the spread of disease

holed up: hidden away

host: the person in charge of a television program who talks with celebrities and other guests

hostess: a woman who entertains guests

house call: a visit by a doctor in someone's home

immigrant (**im** uh grint): a person from one country who moves to settle permanently in another

infirmary (in **furm** uh ree): a place where sick or hurt people are cared for, smaller than a hospital

internship: the period of time that a new doctor spends working with more experienced doctors to prepare to practice medicine on his or her own

involved: taking part in

labor: physical work

legacy (**leg** uh see): what someone leaves behind for future generations after they have died

logging train: train carrying wood that has been sawn into planks

lured: led into a trap, tricked

malnourished (mal **nur** ishd): not having enough food, or not eating the right kinds of food to be healthy

medical license: a certificate that says a person is allowed to practice medicine

medical school: a school one attends to learn to be a doctor

minted: made into money

mission (**mi** shuhn): a special purpose or task

modern: up-to-date or new

muff: a tube-like item of clothing, often lined with fur, that girls put their hands inside to keep warm

murmuring: speaking very quietly

nature: the character of someone or something

netting: fabric that looks like a net, usually used as protection from insects

newsreel: a short film of recent news that played before a movie in a theater started in the 1940s and 1950s

nursing home: a place for the care of the very old or of anyone who needs nursing care over a long period of time

overcome: to deal with or get over a problem or feeling

pediatrician (pee dee uh **trish** uhn): a doctor who takes care of babies and children

pneumonia (nuh **mohn** yuh): a disease that causes the lungs to be filled with fluid, making breathing difficult

practice: to work at a profession, especially as a doctor or lawyer

practice: the business of a doctor or lawyer

prairie (**prair** ree): a large area of flat or rolling grassland with few or no trees

primary (**prI** mair ree): most important

prodding: encouragement or urging

producer: a person in charge of putting on a play or making a movie or television program

profession: a job that requires special education, such as law or medicine

professor: a teacher of the highest rank at a college or university

proposal: an offer of marriage

protective: made to keep someone safe from harm

recovered: got better after illness or injury

requisite (**rek** wuh zit): something someone must do or have; a requirement

resort (ree **zort**): a place where people go for rest and relaxation

role model: a person looked up to for his or her ability or experience

route: the places a doctor or delivery person goes each day in the same order

rural: in the countryside or on a farm

scholarship (**sko** lur ship): money given to help a student continue his or her schooling

seals: stamps with a special design

sedative (**sed** uh tiv): a drug that makes a person sleepy and relaxed

senior (**seen** yur): a student in the final year of high school

sewage (**soo** ij): liquid and solid waste that is carried away in sewers and drains

small talk: talk about unimportant matters

socialite (**soh** shuh lɪt): a person well-known for wearing stylish clothing and giving and attending parties

squab (skwahb): a very young pigeon

square foot: an area twelve inches long and twelve inches wide

statistic (stuh **tis** tik): a fact or piece of information presented in numbers

stethoscope (**ste** thuhs kohp): a medical instrument used by doctors and nurses to listen to the heart, lungs, and other areas

suffocate: to die from lack of oxygen

tenement (**ten** uh mint): a run-down building, especially one that is crowded and in a poor part of a city

tetanus (**tet** nis): an infection in a cut that causes muscles to become stiff and can lead to death

tourism (**tur** iz uhm): traveling and visiting places for pleasure

trolley: an electric streetcar that runs on tracks and gets its power from an overhead wire

unsanitary (uhn **san** i tair ree): not clean; full of germs

unveiled (uhn **vayld**): uncovered, revealed

vaccinated (**vak** si nay ted): given a shot or pill to protect against disease

vaporizer (**vayp** ur iz ur): a machine that can change water or medicine into steam (or vapor) to make breathing easier

venison (**ven** i sin): the meat from a deer

waded: walked through water

washboard: a board with slats used to rub clothes against when washing by hand

Wisconsin National Guard: soldiers who volunteer to serve the state of Wisconsin

Women's Christian Temperance (tem pur ins) **Union:** a group of women that worked together to stop the selling and drinking of beer and liquor in the 1910s

wood-burning stove: a stove that is fueled by wood, often used for both cooking and heating

worldly good: riches or wealth

Reading Group Guide and Activities

Discussion Questions

❖ What 3 adjectives would you pick to describe Dr. Kate? Find an example from the story that supports each word.

❖ Throughout her life, Dr. Kate had to make many difficult decisions. Sometimes, she had to choose between 2 things she really wanted. Look through the story and identify 3 places where Kate had to make a choice. Which choice do you think was the hardest for her to make? Why? What would have been the most difficult for you? Describe a time in your life when you had to make a tough decision.

❖ When Dr. Kate was on the television show *This Is Your Life*, the host invited people from her past to tell about important stages of her life. If you were a featured guest on that program, who are the important people in your life that would tell stories about you? What do you think each would say?

❖ Pretend you lived in 1956 and you've just heard of the Woodruff penny campaign. Write a letter to Dr. Kate and the Million Penny Paraders donating to their collection.

❖ If you were going to collect money for a cause, what cause would you pick? Why?

Activities

❧ Dr. Kate didn't have a lot of high-tech equipment or special medicines to help her patients. She often had to make do with what she had when she cared for her patients in the woods. Research to find out more about first aid and what *you* can do in an emergency. Find out what comes in a first aid kit and how each item is used. Create a poster of first aid tips.

❧ When Dr. Kate first moved to northern Wisconsin and lived in her cabin, it was very simple, like camping. If you were going to spend a week in a cabin in the woods, what would you bring? What if there was no electricity and no bathrooms? Make a list of supplies you would need. Then imagine you've just completed a day of camping and are now sitting around the campfire. Write a journal entry describing your day.

❧ Find out more about Elizabeth Blackwell, the first woman to become a doctor in the United States. Who were some of the other early women doctors? What were some of the special challenges they faced?

❧ With your classmates, choose a cause you would like to raise money for. Then plan your campaign. How much money will you need? Who will you ask, and how will you ask them? Create a plan for your campaign listing each step you'll need to take. Then, write a letter you can send to donors, and make a poster to tell others about your cause.

The penny is America's smallest unit of money, and one of its oldest. Research the history of the penny and write a report using these Web sites:

Americans for Common Cents, www.pennies.org

The MegaPenny Project, www.kokogiak.com/megapenny

Penny Lovers of America, www.pennylovers.org/intro.html

The United States Mint, www.usmint.gov/kids

To Learn More about Becoming a Doctor

Adamson, Heather. *A Day in the Life of a Doctor*. Mankato, Minnesota: Capstone, 2000.

Buckley, James, Jr. *A Day with a Doctor*. Mankato, Minnesota: Child's World, 2007.

Gale, Karen Buhler. *The Kids' Guide to First Aid: All About Bruises, Burns, Stings, Sprains & Other Ouches*. Nashville: Williamson Publishing, 2001.

The Human Body. London: DK Eyewitness Books, 2004.

Leavitt, Amy Jean. *Elizabeth Blackwell*. Hockessin, Delaware: Michell Lane Books, 2008.

Miller, Robin H., M.D. *Kids Ask the Doctor*. New York: Arlington, Texas: Customized Communications, Inc., 2003.

Morley, David. *Healing Our World: Inside Doctors Without Borders*. Toronto: Fitzhenry and Whitestone, 2006.

Robbins, Trina. *Elizabeth Blackwell: The First Woman Doctor*. Mankato, Minnesota: Capstone, 2007.

Acknowledgments

This book began as an idea from a profile on Wisconsin Public Television's *Wisconsin Stories*. I loved the story of a woman doctor in the northwoods and of the schoolchildren who helped out their community. I am also indebted to author Adele Comandini, who saw the heart in Dr. Kate's story and spent time with her, resulting in a very helpful biography, *Dr. Kate: Angel on Snowshoes*, first published in 1956. All quotes in the present volume come from Comandini's book, copyright 1977 by the Doctor Kate Historical Society, Woodruff, Wisconsin. More details were dug out from the Wisconsin Area Research Center Network. Thank you to the Special Collections and Archives staff at the University of Wisconsin-Eau Claire, for requesting materials for me from around the state so that I could examine newspaper clippings, handwritten high school memos, photographs, speech scripts, and more from Dr. Kate's time.

The Dr. Kate Museum staff in Woodruff, Wisconsin, was invaluable. Helen Schlecht, Sue Lindstrom, and Marsha Dowd showed me around, answered questions, filled in questionable dates, and provided photos. These volunteers' memories help to keep Dr. Kate alive. Please stop by and visit them! Also thanks to Joel Heiman, photographer at the Wisconsin Historical Society, for traveling to the museum to scan and shoot the art program. Thanks also to Bobbie Malone, Director of the Office of School Services at the Wisconsin Historical Society, and Sara Phillips, editor at the Wisconsin Historical Society Press, for pulling together the manuscript and photographs and getting them ready for outside eyes to see. Finally, thanks to Eli Wojahn, my research assistant, who tested out Woodruff's local beaches with me, and Cal and Don Wojahn for being such good first readers and listeners. I know I'm not always a "cookie mother" either—thanks for understanding.

Index

This index points you to the pages where you can read about persons, places, and ideas. If you do not find the word you are looking for, try to think of another word that means about the same thing.

When you see a page number in **bold** it means there is a picture on that page.

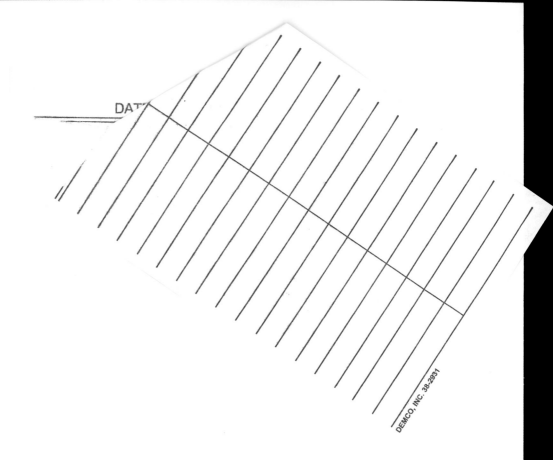

DAT